The Workhouse, Southwell

Nottinghamshire

National Trust

The last resort

Workhouses occupy a dark place in the collective memory of the British. The fear of the very word 'workhouse' still lingers today, when workhouses are a thing of the past. Many are the anecdotes recalling threats ('If you don't behave, you'll end up in the workhouse!') and fears ('My grandmother wouldn't go into hospital, because she was frightened it was a workhouse').

A male dormitory, left as it was found when the National Trust bought The Workhouse in 1997

Workhouses were part of the most ambitious welfare and construction programme ever attempted – the New Poor Law of 1834. This created a network of hundreds of specially designed workhouses, 15–20 miles apart, across the country. Life inside these workhouses was to be basic and dull. The intention was that those who became destitute (paupers) could find shelter there, but those who were not destitute would not ask for the help, knowing that it meant going into the workhouse.

Workhouses would help taxpayers separate the poor who could help themselves from the paupers who would not survive without help. It was accepted that many people were poor. Pauperism was a step beyond that: not knowing where your next meal was coming from, or not having a roof over your head. Even today some think that state benefits encourage people to be lazy and not look for work, while others think they are not generous enough. Politicians debate whether state aid should be tied to work and training, and benefits agencies struggle to provide help to those in need without removing the incentive to work.

The architects of the New Poor Law did not set out to be cruel – only fair and efficient. Yet the workhouse system was an uneasy combination of care and deterrence. Although everyone could be fed, clothed and sheltered within the workhouse, the stigma attached to people who went there, the tedious regime inside it, the hard work, and the rumours (sometimes true) of corrupt staff ensured that it truly was the place of last resort.

Workhouses catered for more than just the unemployed. Many people were destitute through no fault of their own· those without family support; the elderly without work, savings or pensions; children without parents; deserted wives; unmarried mothers and their children; some with mental illness; many with physical disabilities; the sick without carers. All these were offered the workhouse, if their poverty forced them to ask for help.

And so, surprisingly, we see the foundations of modern systems of health, welfare and benefits in the New Poor Law. Many of our modern hospitals and residential homes were literally built on the foundations of workhouses, so that few of the hundreds constructed in the 19th century survive in their original form. The Workhouse at Southwell was not only a pioneer of the new system, but has been little altered since. The National Trust has preserved it so that visitors can see a complete workhouse, feel the sense of enclosure inside the high walls, understand how the functional wings segregated men, women and children, and 'meet' the people who lived and worked here.

The New Poor Law is an announcement ... that whosoever will not work ought not to live. Can the poor man that is willing to work always find work and live by his work? A man willing but unable to find work is ... the saddest thing under the sun.

Thomas Carlyle, 1839

Luke Fildes's *Applicants for Admission to a Casual Ward* (1874) distils the horror of Victorian poverty

Homelessness, pensions, disabilities, unemployment – the New Poor Law tackled social issues that remain with us today

The Old Poor Law

Medieval alms-giving

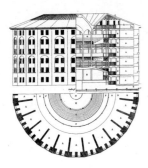

Jeremy Bentham's 'Panopticon, or Inspection-house' of 1791 was designed to provide a building for 'punishing the incorrigible, guarding the insane, reforming the vicious, confining the suspected, employing the idle and maintaining the helpless'. As at The Workhouse, inmates were supervised from a central point

The poor laws go back to Elizabethan times. Before that, there was no state provision for the sick and old, or for the able-bodied pauper who could not find work. Instead, paupers had been supported by their own families and neighbours, by charities, or by the church. This system was disrupted by Henry VIII's Dissolution of the Monasteries in the 1530s and by people moving from the countryside to the towns.

After the Dissolution, several laws were passed to provide work for the poor, shelter for the old and sick, and punishment for vagrants and beggars. At the end of the 16th century, each parish was made responsible for its own poor. The cost of keeping the poor would be paid by a tax on those who owned and occupied property – the 'ratepayers'. They elected parish 'overseers' of the poor, who administered the 'relief', as assistance to the poor became known. This system was consolidated in an Act of 1601, now known as the Old Poor Law. Its main aims were to find work for those who could work, and to shelter those who could not work because of age or disability.

The Old Poor Law survived, with only a few additions, for over 200 years, but during that time the system gradually broke down. Individual parishes tried many ways to contain the increasing cost of the poor rates. One method was to subsidise wages, where they were so low that even those in work still needed help. Another method was to give money or goods that the poor needed such as food or coal. This was known as 'out-relief'. Attempts to make the able-bodied earn this relief often involved groups of labourers carrying out pointless tasks. Such work did not cover the cost of the relief, and it was hard to make people work well under these conditions.

Some parishes set aside buildings for workshops or residential institutions. These were called poorhouses, workhouses or houses of industry. They might provide equipment for working during the day, or somewhere to sleep for those who went out to work during the day and returned at night. Almshouses continued to house the old and helpless, but were paid for by charities rather than taxes.

Public attitudes varied between pitying the poor and blaming their condition on their own idleness and lack of thrift. By the early 19th century, the problem seemed to be out of hand. The total cost of poor relief in England and Wales rose from £4 million to nearly £8 million between 1803 and 1818. This reflected the pressure on poor workers in both towns and rural districts, because of mechanization, enclosure of land, or the rising population. There were riots, as workers felt robbed of their economic freedom. These led to growing unease among the wealthier classes.

The day room of St James's Parish Workhouse in London in 1808. Victorian reformers were concerned at the cost of such 'pauper palaces'

The New Poor Law

The Rev. J.T. Becher, who masterminded The Workhouse. His concern was for 'the moral and temporal welfare of the community', and his other local interests included a lunatic asylum, friendly society for savings and the house of correction

(*Below*) The distant spires of Southwell Minster glimpsed from The Workhouse emphasise its isolated setting

Parliament and reformers constantly discussed schemes to change and improve the poor laws. A Royal Commission was set up to investigate the administration of the poor laws across the country. Nottinghamshire reformers provided some interesting experiments for the Commissioners to study at Nottingham, Bingham and a group of parishes around Southwell, which had formed the Thurgarton Hundred Incorporation.

In 1828 the founder of the Incorporation, the Rev. John Thomas Becher, wrote a pamphlet called *The Antipauper System*. This explained how he had first experimented with a small workhouse for the parish of Southwell itself, and, assisted by the overseer George Nicholls, brought the poor rates down by 75% in three years. Becher then encouraged 49 surrounding parishes to pool their resources and copy his scheme on a larger and more efficient scale. In

1824 they agreed to build a new workhouse in open fields just outside Southwell, which is now in the care of the National Trust.

Becher's pamphlet publicised the success of this new Incorporated Workhouse in reducing the poor rates and 'improving the moral demeanour' of the poor by housing them in a specially designed new building that was meant to act as a deterrent. The Commission held it up as the best example in its report, which led to the Poor Law Amendment Act of 1834, known as the New Poor Law.

Many of the ideas Becher used had been tried elsewhere, but it was the way in which he combined them that provided the prototype for New Poor Law workhouses. The Southwell example continued to influence the new national system after Nicholls was appointed one of three Commissioners responsible for setting up and running the system in 1834. It became Southwell Union Workhouse in 1836.

(*Right*) Built as Thurgarton Hundred Incorporated Workhouse in 1824, The Workhouse became Southwell Union Workhouse in 1836

Main features of the new system

- Many parishes combined into unions, covering a radius of about ten miles, to build cost-effective workhouses for the poor of their area. By 1839, almost 600 unions were operating in England and Wales.

- The workhouse would be the only option offered to most who applied for relief. (In practice, more people were helped outside the workhouse than in.)

- The workhouse regime would deter through the principles of supervision, classification and segregation.

- New workhouses were designed to embody these principles.

- A small paid staff headed by a Governor, or Master, and Matron would run each workhouse.

- Staff were responsible to a committee of unpaid ratepayers, known as Guardians, elected from each parish.

- Able-bodied paupers would be made to carry out menial and arduous labour, but this would not be for profit.

- The old and infirm would also be housed, but not given the same strict regime of work.

From Overseer at Southwell, George Nicholls rose to become a Poor Law Commissioner and later introduced the New Poor Law to Ireland

Sampson Kempthorne designed model workhouses for the new unions to copy. This one for 300 paupers has many similarities to the Southwell prototype

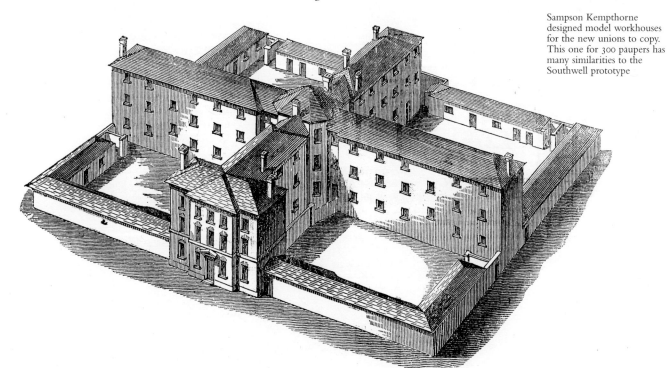

Staff

Jessie Phillips, the heroine of Fanny Trollope's 1844 novel of that name, faints while being interviewed for admission to a workhouse by the Board of Guardians. The Guardians met weekly in the Committee Room to discuss finance and staff, and to decide who should be admitted or receive assistance at home

Workhouse Guardians were elected by the local ratepayers

Workhouse staff had strict rules to follow, and very little power to change them, but they still managed to stamp their personalities on the institutions they ran.

The staff was headed by the Master, who reported to elected, unpaid Guardians. These in turn were responsible to the ratepayers who funded the poor laws, but also to the local Poor Law Assistant Commissioner, who reported back to the Poor Law Commissioners at Somerset House in London. All these posts were held by men. The Matron supervised nursing, cooking, cleaning, laundry and the care of women and children. From 1858 Louisa Twining, of the tea family, campaigned to improve standards in workhouses, and later some female Guardians were elected.

The link between the Poor Law Commissioners and the local unions

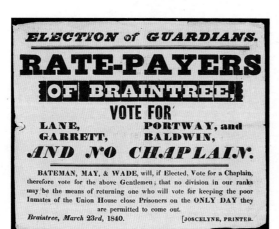

was the small team of Assistant Commissioners, later called Poor Law Inspectors. These seventeen hardworking men first established the unions and their workhouses and then travelled round large regions, inspecting and reporting back on how well they were abiding by the new regulations.

The Guardians

At the head of the local hierarchy were the Guardians. (The closest modern equivalent are District or County Councillors.) They were elected annually from among the ratepayers. For many, it was an onerous duty; for some, a chance to do good; for a few, an opportunity to exploit the system to benefit their own business. Some were aristocrats like Lord Manvers, but most were local farmers or businessmen.

The Guardians' Clerk was a well-paid position, often taken by an aspiring young solicitor or another professional man. The Clerk was not resident but came and took minutes at the meetings and corresponded with other Boards of Guardians and with the Commissioners in London. His records help us to understand how the workhouses functioned.

Other union staff who reported directly to the Guardians were the Relieving Officers, of whom there were two for the Southwell Union. Staff who attended about once a week included the Chaplain and the Medical Officer. These might also be questioned by the Inspector about standards of care in 'the house'.

he last meeting of Southwell Board of Guardians, March 21st 1930

The Master and Matron

The most important member of staff was the Master. He had day-to-day responsibility for the institution, and the Guardians blamed him if things went wrong. Many of the first Masters in the new workhouses of the 1830s and '40s came from the armed forces, reflecting the controlling and enforcing role they were expected to have.

The Master was often seen as cruel and corrupt. In Dickens's *Oliver Twist*, he is depicted as starving the younger inmates. The 'Andover Scandal' of 1845 showed that this actually happened. After the Master of the Andover Union Workhouse failed to give the working men the food they were entitled to, they were found hungrily gnawing at the old, green bones they were meant to be grinding for fertiliser. This caused a huge scandal and a revision of the whole system, so it certainly was not the normal behaviour expected of a workhouse Master. Masters, like the rest of us, were probably a mixture of the cruel and kind, efficient and inefficient. It was up to the Guardians and Inspectors to spot and dismiss the bad ones.

The Master had to complete many different forms and ledgers, and by the end of the 19th century his role was becoming increasingly administrative. Poor Law examinations were set up so that workhouse staff became qualified administrators, in the same way as the head of a hospital might be.

Mr and Mrs Willatt were Master and Matron at Southwell in the 1920s. Ambitious poor law staff made the right marriage. A Porter, Clerk or Assistant Master stood a good chance of promotion, if his wife had nursing qualifications. But if the spouse failed, so did the career. When Master Willatt died in 1931, Matron left, and a new couple took their places

In 1845 inmates at the Andover Workhouse were given so little food that they resorted to gnawing bones meant for fertiliser

This Necessaries and Miscellaneous Account Book from the 1890s was found in the roof. It records the many cleaning materials used to keep The Workhouse clean and the inmates busy

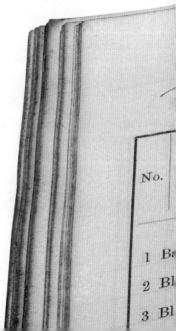

No.

1 Ba

2 Bl

3 Bl

The Matron was responsible for the care and supervision of the women and children and for nursing duties at a time when nursing qualifications did not exist. At first, she was simply the wife of the Master, with no formal qualifications for the job. As nursing standards rose, so these came to be expected of the Matron.

The Schoolteacher

The Schoolteacher's lot was an unenviable one, and there was a high turnover of teaching staff. The work was badly paid and of low status, but reasonable standards were expected by school inspectors. Southwell Union employed couples for teaching at first, but later simply employed a single Schoolmistress. This was usually a live-in job that entailed supervising the children throughout the day as well as instructing them in the classroom. At Southwell, the Master and Matron assisted with teaching, probably because the Schoolmistress could not teach girls and boys, and different age groups, separately. The Education Act of 1870 ensured schooling for everyone, and it was with relief that the Southwell Union Guardians abolished the school in 1885, sending workhouse children to local schools instead.

(*Right*) 'Oliver Twist asks for more' – the most famous attack on the New Poor Law system. In fact, workhouses gave the poorest children an education and food that many would not otherwise have received

W. Fryer Ma

3rd Week of the

(Master. No. 20.)

Southwell UNION.

CESSARIES AND MISCELLANEOUS ACCOUNT for the

RTICLES.	STOCK BROUGHT FORWARD.	NEW STOCK.	No. of Invoice.	TOTALS OF STOCK BROUGHT FORWARD AND NEW STOCK.	By the Paupers.	By the Officers and Servants of the Workhouse.	W
				8			
				.8			.2
icks...	8			5			
..	.8			.13			
d ... lbs.	5						
lbs.	.13			3			
				2			

CONSUMED

Getting in

The Workhouse stairs kept the various categories of inmate apart

C.W. Cope's *Poor Law Guardians, Board Day, Application for Bread* (1841) was based on a meeting of the Staines Union Guardians

Vagrants queuing for admittance to a workhouse for the night. The vagrants' wards for Southwell Union were demolished in the 20th century

There was more than one way into a workhouse. In an emergency, the destitute could arrive at the gate and be admitted by the Master to the receiving or casual wards. Here they awaited the next Guardians' Committee meeting. It was more usual for them to apply for assistance through one of the union's Relieving Officers. Each of these officers travelled through their part of the union weekly. This meant applicants for relief had a regular, advertised local time and place to put their case. Some might need help due to sickness in the family; others might be abandoned children or mothers. Often applicants were simply unable to cope

with the costs of rent, food, fuel and clothing. Travelling vagrants who came from outside the union and only stayed overnight queued for admittance by five or six in the evening and were discharged after completing a specified amount of work the next day.

A Relieving Officer was obliged to assist urgent cases immediately, for example finding medical assistance, or giving vouchers to pay for food or other necessities. Less immediate cases would be presented at the weekly meeting of the Guardians. Sometimes the officer would present these cases to the Guardians, and sometimes paupers would put their own cases. Those applying for relief would hope that they might be given some money or other assistance that would enable them to continue living at home. Often, however, they were told, 'No order except the workhouse'. The Guardians strove to balance the pressure to keep costs down against the duty, and often the desire, to provide decent humane treatment. They were expected to enforce the laws offering only the workhouse to 'able-bodied persons and their families'.

A typical case

14 Dec 1845 I hereby certify that Jos Worthington residing at Halem is suffering from Rheumatism and other infirmities and incapable of work, he is able to be removed to the workhouse

Wm Holland Surgeon

Once applicants had been admitted to the receiving ward, they were separated into men, women and children. They would then be searched, undressed and washed. Objects such as cards, dice, 'spiritous liquors' and matches were confiscated. Clothes and other objects were cleaned (often literally fumigated) and ticketed with their owner's details, ready to be returned on departure. Inmates would wear workhouse uniforms during their stay.

New inmates waited in the receiving wards until the Medical Officer inspected and classified them. At Southwell, the Inspector found these wards 'insufficiently furnished' and with no suitable lavatories. Once categorised as able-bodied, infirm, or sometimes lunatic, or sick, they could join others of the same category within the main workhouse building or the infirmary, and enter the daily routine. Medical Officers often found they were admitting the sick, who could be granted relief at home, but perhaps had no one to care for them, and so workhouses increasingly provided hospitals for the poor.

Getting out

In theory, inmates could be discharged from the workhouse, if considered capable of supporting themselves. However, compulsory discharges of inmates were rare and could be ordered only by the Guardians. According to the regulations, 'Any pauper may quit the Workhouse upon giving to the Master … a reasonable notice of his wish to do so; and… the whole of [his] family shall be sent with him.' This rule was intended to prevent children being abandoned in workhouses. Many of the able-bodied came in only for a short period, and left again when work was available. Children were often apprenticed out of the workhouse at twelve or thirteen.

Clothing and belongings were ticketed with their owner's details, ready to be returned on departure

(*Left*) Inmates were washed before being issued with uniforms

Vagrants received a meal and a bed for the night

Inmates

Able-bodied inmates in the 1920s

The old and infirm were a very mixed group, not all elderly. They often stayed in workhouses for years while the able-bodied came and went more quickly

There were seven different categories, or 'classes', into which workhouse inmates were divided:

1. Old and infirm men
2. Able-bodied men
3. Boys, 7–12 (later 7–15)
4. Old and infirm women
5. Able-bodied women
6. Girls, 7–15
7. Children under 7

Able-bodied

The different categories had several different names. The able-bodied were also called the 'idle and profligate' or the 'undeserving poor', which gives an idea of attitudes to the unemployed. The terms really meant anyone considered physically capable of working who was not, regardless of whether this was due to their own incompetence, laziness or lack of training; or, more commonly, to general levels of unemployment and scarcity of work. Work was seasonal in agricultural areas like Southwell Union, so The Workhouse filled up during the winter. There were also longer periods of recession, such as the 1840s, which put pressure on workhouse space for a number of years.

It was the able-bodied who performed the 'work' from which workhouses took their name. The idea was that work inside a workhouse would be harder than jobs outside so that the workhouse would not be a soft option for those who did not want to work hard.

Female able-bodied paupers also came because they had lost their jobs or because their husbands were out of work. Having a large number of children could stretch family resources beyond the limit, even if the husband was earning some wages. Some were single mothers. Although the Poor Law Commissioners disapproved of the former practice of forcing them to wear a distinctive 'disgraceful dress', these women were still shunned by others.

Old and infirm

Other names for this class were 'blameless' or 'deserving' poor. These were mainly people who could no longer work due to age-related disabilities, although they might have worked all their lives. Some would have lived in cottages 'tied' to their job and so lost their home with their income. Younger people with disabilities were also included in this category. Dickens mentions an example of a huntsman paralysed in a fall and left to live out his

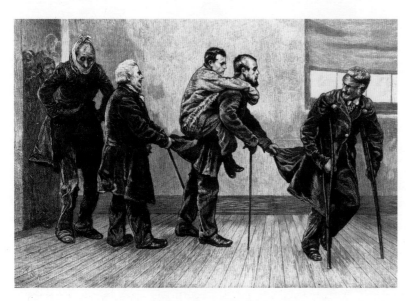

days in the workhouse. Some mental disabilities were recognised and sufferers classed as 'lunatic' or 'idiot', who might be allowed 'blameless' status, and did not have to work. Milder cases (called 'imbeciles') often worked with the able-bodied. Violent 'lunatics' were sent to the asylum in Nottingham. Many of the blameless poor were those without families to support them. Although couples might be admitted, it was more common for an elderly person to find they needed help after their spouse had died, so there were many unattached people in workhouses.

Children

Children entered the workhouse for several reasons. Many came in with a parent or parents. There was also a large number of orphan children, whose relations were too poor to support them. Some children who appeared to be orphans were actually the abandoned offspring of parents who could not afford to keep them and had fled to find work in a different part of the country. Legal steps were taken to trace these parents and make them responsible for their offspring. Some children were born in the workhouse after their mothers arrived pregnant. Although children were separated from parents, as these 'undeserving' poor were considered a bad influence, brothers or sisters might stay together, depending on how they fitted into the separate categories of children up to seven years, and of boys and girls over seven.

Vagrants

Separate from the seven categories of inmates were the casuals, tramps or 'sturdy' vagrants, who were the travellers of the road. The majority were male, but there were women too. They would travel the country, queuing up at the nearest workhouse on the appointed hour in the evening for a meal and a bed. Often they would hide any personal belongings or money before going into the workhouse. After performing a set quantity of work, they were free to move on. They would often work in a circuit, walking from one workhouse to the next and eventually back to the first again. Some workhouses were to be avoided, if the Master was very harsh or the food particularly bad. Vagrants drew maps for each other or left signs to warn their fellow travellers. Many still remember these travellers stopping at private houses to do an odd job or boil a kettle.

This anti-Poor Law cartoon in *Punch* shows a mother being separated from her child. The Poor Law Orders allowed mothers access to children under seven 'at all reasonable times'

Female workhouse inmates in 1884

Workhouse as built in 1824

Legend:
- Able-bodied men
- Old and infirm men
- Able-bodied women
- Old and infirm women
- Children
- Staff
- Guardians
- Functional Areas

1 Entrance Porch
2 Committee Room
3 School Room
4 Master's Room
5 Master's Staircase
6 Clerk's Office
7 Kitchen
8 Scullery
9 Back Entrances
10 Women's Day Room
11 Women's Day Room
12 Women's Staircases
13 Women's Exercise Courts
14 Privies
15 Men's Day Room
16 Men's Day Room
17 Men's Staircases
18 Men's Exercise Courts
19 Washing Benches
20 Back Court (women's)
21 Back Court (men's)
22 Porter's Lodge
23 Tool House
24 Stable
25 Ashes House (women's)
26 Bath Room
27 Wash House
28 Coal Yard (replaced by Laundry)
29 Bake House
30 Store Room
31 Ashes House (men's)
32 Cow House
33 Dead Room
34 Punishment Cell
35 Master's Bed Room
36 Master's Staircase
37 Water Closet
38 Women's Dormitories
39 Men's Dormitories
40 Children's Dormitories
41 Receiving Ward
42 Mangle Room
43 Infirmary
44 Nurse's Apartment
45 New School Room (National Trust reception)
46 New Laundry

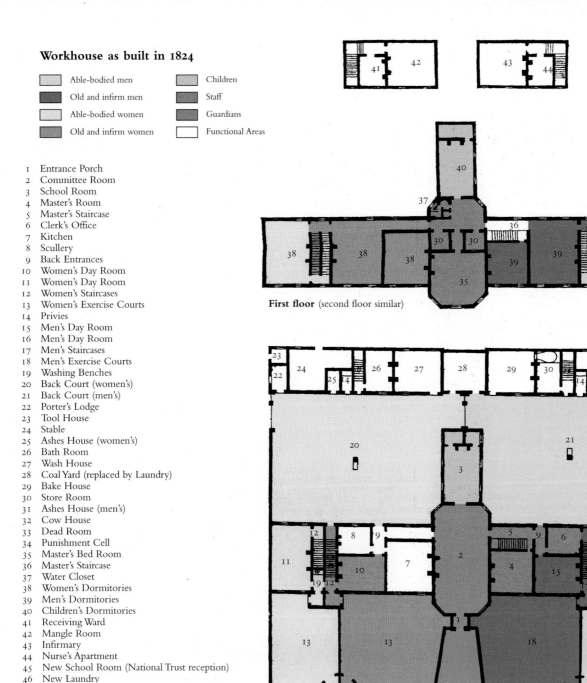

First floor (second floor similar)

Ground floor

Workhouse as restored

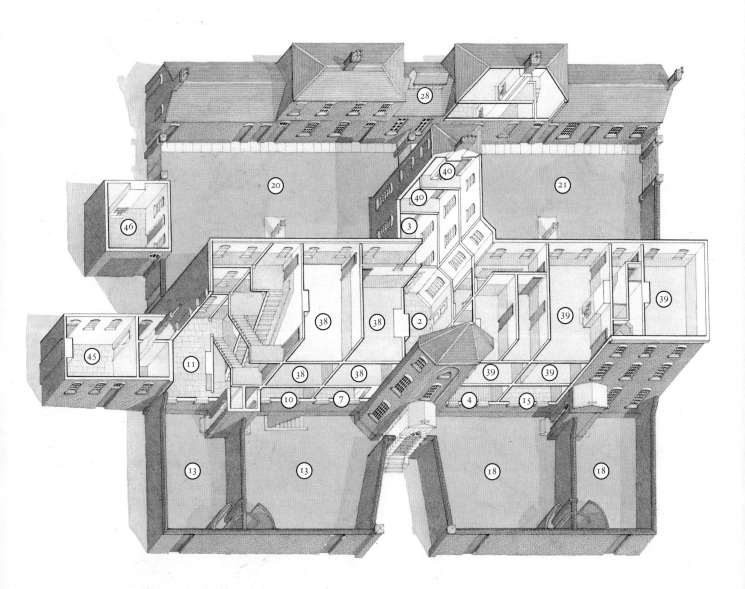

Life in the workhouse in the mid-19th century

This advertisement shows the need for strong beds. Those at Southwell had straw mattresses, which the Inspector often found soggy and dirty

Poor Law Commissioners' model timetable of 1835

6am (7 in winter)	Workhouse rising bell
6.30 (7.30 in winter)	Breakfast, preceded by prayers
7 (8 in winter)	Work until 12
12	Dinner
1	Work again until supper
6	Supper
8	Followed by more prayers and then bed

The daily routine of inmates was dictated by daylight. They rose and went to bed early so as not to waste the ratepayers' money on candles or lamp oil. The rising bell rang at 6 when the days were long, and at 7 from October to March. The coal fire would have taken the edge off the winter cold, but the dormitories were designed to allow plenty of air to circulate so draughts from the ventilation panels and from the windows would have made mornings chilly. Paupers rose, and exchanged their night-shirts for the uniform, which hung on a peg overnight. There were no cupboards in the dormitories, as the paupers would have had few possessions to put in them.

The morning routine included making the beds and taking chamber-pots used in the night downstairs for emptying (later earth-closets were installed). Having gone downstairs for breakfast, inmates were not permitted back to the dormitories during the day, unless cleaning them was one of their duties.

There was a roll-call of paupers, then prayers and a breakfast of bread and gruel. All meals were taken in the different day rooms in this workhouse, although most Victorian workhouses usually had one large dining room for all inmates.

A ward at Chorlton Union Hospital near Manchester in 1865

(Right) Workhouse diets varied little locally. This dietary from neighbouring Basford Union includes cheese for the men but Southwell Guardians replaced the cheese with extra milk

(Opposite) This dormitory was subdivided in the 19th century, perhaps to make extra space for the sick or because new rules allowed elderly married couples to share a bedroom

Dietary for Able-bodied Men and Women.

		Breakfast		Dinner					Supper		
		Bread	Porridge	Meat	Potatoes	Bread	Soup	Suet Pudding	Bread	Cheese	Porridge
		oz	pts	oz	lbs	oz	pts	oz	oz	oz	pts
Sunday	Men	7	1½	7	1½	-	"	"	8	2	"
	Women	6	1¼	5	1	-	"	"	6	1½	"
Monday	Men	7	1½	"	"	4	2	"	7	"	1½
	Women	6	1½	"	"	3	1½	"	6	"	1½
Tuesday	Men	7	1½	"	"	"	"	16	7	"	1½
	Women	6	1½	"	"	"	"	14	6	"	1½
Wednesday	Men	7	1½	"	*	4	2	"	7	"	1½
	Women	6	1½	"	"	3	1½	"	6	"	1½
Thursday	Men	7	1½	7	1½	"	"	"	7	"	1½
	Women	6	1½	5	1	"	"	"	6	"	1½
Friday	Men	7	1½	"	"	4	2	"	7	"	1½
	Women	6	1½	"	"	3	1½	"	6	"	1½
Saturday	Men	7	1½	"	"	"	"	16	7	"	1½
	Women	6	1½	"	"	"	"	14	6	"	1¼

Work

Those who could work had a busy morning. Work for the men involved breaking stones for roads and old bones for fertiliser, unpicking old rope (called 'oakum'), turning a mill handle, and household duties such as decorating. There was also much digging, as the male inmates worked the garden. It would have been kept neat and functional, with the orchard in front of the building and vegetable plots bordered with low box

Oakum was lengths of old tarred rope, such as these fragments found in the roof of The Workhouse

hedges. This supplied many of the potatoes and other vegetables eaten by the inmates. The women carried out cooking, laundry, cleaning – scrubbing the stone floors or doing back-breaking washing – spinning, knitting and needlework, and picking oakum. Some of the work helped the workhouse run more economically, but as its main aim was to deter, it often served no useful purpose.

There was no cut-off age for work, as inmates were simply 'kept employed according to their capacity and ability'. So quite elderly inmates would work. However, for the oldest or very disabled inhabitants, the 'blameless poor', more time was spent in the day rooms, if they could manage the steep stairs from the sleeping rooms. Here the hours might be whiled away on wooden chairs or benches, with perhaps some religious texts as reading matter and, in winter, a small coal fire. They could also go out into the exercise yard for air, where there may also have been benches. For the very weak and infirm, daily life might have been confined to their sleeping room, tended by inmate nurses.

Able-bodied inmates picking oakum, traditionally used for caulking ships. This was very hard on the fingers

Education

While the adults were working, the children were supervised by the Schoolmaster and Schoolmistress. The formal education in workhouses was subject to official inspection long before education was compulsory for children outside. The boys and girls between seven and fifteen were divided into different classes for school, while the infants were taught together. The principle was that 'all children in the workhouse shall be trained to habits of usefulness, industry, and virtue'. The basics of arithmetic, reading and writing were taught, but some workhouse schools also aspired to teach geography, more complex mathematics and singing 'very pleasingly in parts'. The Chaplain gave religious instruction.

Classroom education occupied three hours a day, while the rest was spent on 'industrial training', which meant teaching the children how to work. For the boys, this could entail working in the garden, while the girls might do needlework, cookery or laundry. The Poor Law

Inspectors disapproved of the lack of separate facilities to teach the children. In a small workhouse like Southwell, it was hard to separate the girls learning laundry skills from the women who were working in the laundry. One Inspector reported, 'The education of girls must always remain morally defective, so long as they are exposed to the many corrupting influences of the workhouse.' There was also time to play: toys such as hoops were ordered, and gifts of toys also came from local benefactors. The Guardians sometimes gave approval for the schoolteacher to take the children on a trip to Lincoln or Derby.

The frosted glass may have been put in to prevent children being distracted by adult inmates in the yard below

Stone-breaking

Old women taking tea in their day room in the Westminster Union Workhouse in 1878

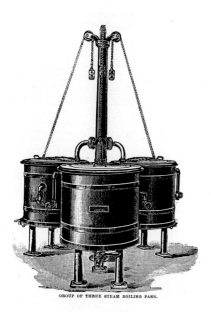

GROUP OF THREE STEAM BOILING PANS.

Large pans were always boiling in the kitchen. Ada Pointen, who worked at The Workhouse in the 1920s, remembers the constant smell of boiled cabbage

The Master recorded punishments in this book. The Guardians inspected it, occasionally reminding him not to overreach his authority

No. of the Case.	NAME.	OFFENCE.	Date of Offence.	Punishment inflicted by Master or other Officer.
90	Mary Ann Cox	Striking the Inmates	Feb 3rd 1864	Taken before Magistrates
91	Ann Warriner Sarah Slater	Fighting Warriner had 2 very bad Black eyes	1864 May 14th	taken before the board
92	Hannah Stickling	Using obscene and profane language & annoying the other inmates	1864 Oct 9th	5 Hours in the refractory Ward
93	John Fox & William Crooks	Fighting	Nov 18th	Stopped their Meat at dinner
94	Sarah Watkins & Ann Warriner	Quarreling and persist in making a great noise when ordered to be silent by the Master	Nov 19th	Stopped their Meal at dinner They are two very disagreable women
95	Henry Stanley	For going away in the House Clothes	1865 June 16th	Stopped his meat at dinner
96	Maria Daley	Using obscene language	1866 Jan 11th	Stopped her meat at Dinner
97	Maria Daley	Cruel treatment to her child and destroying the property of the Board	Jan 16th	Stopped her meat at dinner
98	William Crooks	going away in the house clothes & taking one of the Idiots with him shrun	March 15	
99	William Crooks	wilfully disturb the Inmates at prayers	March 17	
100	William Crooks	going to Upton begging Behaving very indecent to one of the Female Inmates and abusing Dr. Cook	April 10 " 11	Taken before Magistrates

22

Dinner

A morning of work or schooling was followed by an hour for dinner, the main meal of the day. This was boiled meat, peas and potatoes some days and soup on other days. On a Saturday it was simply suet pudding. It may sound bland to modern tastes, but the food was considerably better than many had received before coming to The Workhouse. It was reasonably nutritious, although a little short of Vitamin C. Food was carefully weighed out so that each inmate had no more or less than they were entitled to. Working men received the largest measure of food, the youngest children the least.

Dinner was followed by more hours of work, with only supper to look forward to – it was the same as breakfast. In the time between supper and bedtime came a rare chance for some to relax. A former pauper recalled his first night at a workhouse in the 1830s:

When work was done we had a large room with a good fire and sat round it, some talking of the days gone by and wondering where the end of this poverty would take us, others were singing or making a poor half-witted man sing.

Punishment

Those who were caught misbehaving might find their day rather different. Anyone who swore or threatened another, or refused to work or to wash, might be 'deemed disorderly'. The punishment for this was having bread, potatoes or rice instead of the usual meal. However, if an inmate repeatedly offended, or damaged the building or contents (including graffiti), they were considered 'refractory', and the Guardians could order them to be put in solitary confinement for up to 24 hours. Such punishments were very much controlled by the Guardians rather than the Master to avoid abuse. Children were not to be confined, and there were strict regulations on the beating that was allowed for some male children. In very severe cases, such as the theft of the Guardians' property, or injury to another, paupers could be sent before the magistrates. This happened at Southwell when a persistent offender actually broke down the door of the Refractory Cell in which he had been confined!

Days of rest

There were more pleasant changes from routine. Good Friday and Christmas Day were days of rest. At Christmas, the Guardians authorised a Christmas Dinner of roast beef and plum pudding. On Sundays, only necessary household work was performed and the Chaplain's service was held in the Committee Room.

Visitors

Workhouse inmates, especially the more infirm, who were there for some time, were permitted to receive visitors, usually on a fixed day of the week. If they had family who would visit them, they were allowed small gifts, although not of forbidden items like dice or liquor. Inmates could also request meetings with other family members, such as children, in the workhouse. The visits probably also took place in the Committee Room, supervised by the Master or Matron. Inmates too could request visits out, if they gave reasonable notice.

A workhouse funeral returned deceased paupers to their parishes

View of the rebuilt outside privies from the Master's room

Later history

The men's sleeping room

The nursing staff at Southwell had greatly increased by the 1920s

Through the 1840s and 1850s, workhouses continued to operate along the lines laid down by the 1834 Act, but the poor laws and workhouses were never static. Regulations changed, so did the ways of interpreting them. In 1847 the three Poor Law Commissioners were replaced by a Poor Law Board after an enquiry into the Andover scandal. This Board was succeeded by the Local Government Board in 1871, when the health and sanitation of institutions had come to the fore. Through the century, the focus shifted from deterring the able-bodied from the workhouse, to providing shelter and nursing for those who could never be in work. This laid the groundwork for the Welfare State introduced in 1948.

The change is demonstrated by the ratio of staff to inmates. In 1836 there were four members of staff to an average of 135 inmates. By 1900 there were fewer than 80 inmates on average, and extra staff such as a Porter, a Nurse and Assistant Nurse had joined. Seamstresses, laundry maids, cooks and gardeners soon followed, performing many of the duties that inmates had once done.

Furniture also improved, as chairs with arms and backs replaced plain benches, nursing mothers gained rocking chairs, and chamber-pots were replaced with earth-closets and eventually flushing water-closets. Indulgences such as tobacco for men and snuff for women were introduced, often used as extra treats for inmates who helped, where formerly it had been stipulated that there should be no reward for extra work. Such changes were often suggested by visitors, who might include the Workhouse Visiting Society, established in 1858 to improve conditions in workhouses.

Changing standards entailed alterations to the earlier buildings. The addition of a large infirmary building, completed in 1871, is typical of workhouse development across the country. Changes didn't just benefit inmates. At Southwell, in 1913, the Guardians agreed on new stables to house their six horses and two cars during committee meetings.

By 1900 most of the unemployed poor were receiving help at home, while only the 'mentally deficient', the elderly, unmarried mothers and children and vagrants remained in the workhouses. A Royal Commission in 1905–9 considered that it was no longer appropriate to house all the destitute in one building. Children were already being housed in special homes or even boarded out with families. The introduction of the Old Age Pension in 1909 meant fewer of those who were

simply poor due to age needed to fear the workhouse. The tendency was increasingly to create more specialised homes for different categories or to house them at home.

In 1913 workhouses were renamed 'institutions', but mainly used less stigmatised names. Southwell Union Workhouse became Greet House, after the River Greet that runs below it. Nursing standards continued to rise, and workhouses often provided specialist care for the chronically sick. A new hospital at Greet House in 1926 treated patients with cancer or tuberculosis, and a modern, hygienic mortuary was added.

'The worst street in London': Grays Inn Road in 1904, when urban poverty was still as bad as ever

Ada Pointen, when she was Assistant Matron at Southwell in the 1920s. Her memories have helped us understand the later history of The Workhouse

Staff and residents about 1936

(*Right*) Children and their nurse at Southwell in the 1920s before they moved to 'cottage homes'. Today, very few Nottinghamshire children live in residential homes

From Poor Law to Welfare State

The Local Government Act of 1929 brought an end to the term 'poor law' and passed authority for the former workhouses from the Guardians to the local authorities. Any children remaining in these institutions were moved to specialist homes. Although intended as an improvement, such a change often meant that they saw their parents less than before. After 1929 some former workhouses became municipal hospitals, while others continued under the title Public Assistance Institution. The latter, which included Southwell, still segregated inmates by sex and age, and those who could were still expected to work.

The Welfare State that came into being in 1948 was as radical as the New Poor Law of 1834. It gave unprecedented access to financial benefits and health care to many, such as the unemployed or the elderly poor, once cared for in workhouses. Many former workhouse sites were brought into the new National Health Service as state hospitals, although help still had to be found for those who needed residential care. Vagrants also still gravitated towards former workhouses and had to be found shelter for the night. Often the former inmates (now called 'residents' or 'patients') continued to live in the same buildings, but under the new regime. These became long-stay wards and specialist residential homes for the elderly and those with mental disabilities.

At Greet House, after 1948 former elderly residents were moved into the two infirmaries – first one for men and one for women, later as specialist care for women only. The main workhouse building at Greet House continued to provide accommodation for staff and kitchens for residents' food and later for 'meals on wheels'. However, the women's wing was used until 1977 by the council as temporary homeless accommodation in 'bed-sits' for mothers and children awaiting more permanent housing. The Victorian buildings seemed increasingly unsuitable for modern care, especially the many staircases and the large wards. In the early 1990s a new home was specially built on another site, and the last residents and staff moved away.

One of the rooms used as temporary council accommodation in the 1970s, as found in 1997

Rescue and repair

Peeling back layers of history in The Workhouse's decoration

Excavation revealed the bases of privies exactly as Becher's original plan showed them

Repairing the roof of The Workhouse

When the last residents moved away from The Workhouse, the main building finally moved out of public hands as it was sold for development into apartments. This meant that the building was left empty for some time and fell into disrepair. A survey by the Royal Commission on the Historical Monuments of England revealed that many former workhouses were in a similar state, and recognised that The Workhouse at Southwell was 'the best preserved workhouse standing in England'. Believing the building deserved to be saved, the National Trust decided to buy it. Much research and planning was done, and a grant of £2.25 million from the Heritage Lottery Fund, matched by National Trust fundraising, secured the future of The Workhouse.

The Trust's approach has been to restore missing features, but not to remove elements from the building's later workhouse history. So an early 20th-century laundry block was kept, where Becher had originally put a yard for the coal for the fires. However, more recent changes, such as stud wall partitions and modern windows, have been reversed.

Some elements were missing completely and needed re-creating to return to the full Workhouse plan. Amazingly, some of the original exercise yard walls survived, although remembered as 'garden walls'. Missing sections were replaced. Excavation of these yards revealed that the bases of the privies marked on Becher's plan survived. Archaeology and research concluded that the stone holes at ground level were convenient for emptying chamber-pots as well as being for daytime use. A stone, rather than wooden, privy allowed these to remain unroofed without rotting, and so the privies have been restored without roofs.

Excavation of the tarmacked yards did not reveal the original surface. Perhaps it was stone that was removed, or simply scattered cinders. Records from the 1860s show the Poor Law Inspector requesting that the yards be 're-asphalted', and so a 19th-century asphalt surface has been re-created.

The most ambitious re-creation of a missing element was the west end of the Rear Range. The former Wash House, Entrance Lodge and Receiving Ward were demolished in the 20th century and had been tarmacked over. Archaeologists lifting the tarmac found all the evidence for the original building, which was recorded before the rebuild started over the footprint of the original. The re-created range allows visitors to feel suitably enclosed in the entrance yard. As a modern building, it also allowed us to put modern services and displays here rather than disrupting the surviving 19th-century structure.

The Workhouse in 1997, before the National Trust restored the roof and exercise yard walls

The interior

Most of the original cast-iron window frames survive, although some needed small repairs. The few modern windows were removed and replaced with new iron windows to match the originals. Broken glass was replaced with glass only 2–3mm thick, from Poland, where they can still make glass with the irregularities and variation found in the 19th century. Stone sills of the same local Mansfield White stone were tooled to match the originals.

Very little workhouse furniture survives, so it was not possible to refurnish the building with pieces from the same period. Reproduction furniture in an original space would have jarred and diminished the authenticity of the setting. We felt that the architecture of the building, the reason for its preservation, was strong enough to tell the story on its own. What was really important here were not furnishings, but the people who lived here. That was what distinguished one dormitory from another. So an audio tour, based on the archives, was created to re-people the rooms with sound. The period chosen was the mid-19th century, when most workhouses were complete and functioning under the new system.

While the original furniture had long gone, much of the decoration survived, hidden under later layers. Analysis of paint samples showed how, at first, layers of grey/white distemper were applied onto the bare brick walls regularly, perhaps every year, by the inmates. Distemper is cheap, but also quite soft and powdery, so by the mid-19th century the lower halves of the walls were being painted with an oil-based paint that was more hard-wearing.

The cellar needed little restoration apart from repairing rotting doorways

The colours seen in The Workhouse now come from this period, apart from those in the top-floor men's wing, which appear to date from the early 20th century and which have been left as the National Trust found them in 1997. These rooms were later used for storage and so seem to have escaped redecoration and modernisation of the fireplaces. The surviving grates here were the models for the rest of The Workhouse, where 20th-century fire surrounds had been installed.

The paupers' walls are simply painted brick, but the more 'polite' areas were plastered, and had more sophisticated doors and fireplaces. These were reinstated or repaired with traditional materials. In some rooms, the 20th-century staff had moved into pauper rooms and plastered the walls. This caused damage to the original brick faces, which were revealed and then re-formed by skilled bricklayers.

Some of the upstairs sleeping rooms have been left unrestored

Paint analysis helped us to decorate most of The Workhouse with its mid-19th-century colours. Tooled stone flags were restored to the ground floor

The legacy of the workhouse

The workhouse system may have gone, but are we in a position to condemn it? The workhouse housed such a variety of people under one roof that it was perhaps inevitable that it failed to solve the complex problems associated with poverty.

The problem of the homeless remains unsolved

Today, in contrast, many different state bodies administer pensions, public housing, residential homes and schemes such as Jobseeker's Allowance and Welfare to Work. Issues of work and pensions are separate from care for children and housing. Charities continue to play a major role in providing care and influencing policy.

Ways of offering help to the poor are also more positive. Rather than provide a deterrent incentive to work, modern measures concentrate on training to equip people for work. To a great extent, the stigma of receiving help has also lifted. Many have been lifted out of poverty, thanks to vastly improved health services, employment rights, pensions and education.

There have been huge advances in standards of care, and in expectations, since workhouses were phased out. However, those who worked in the old system will point out its advantages. A former Relieving Officer of the 1930s and '40s remembers his constitutional duty to help anyone in need, 'The greatest thing that bothers me in my old age is to see people sitting begging because in the days of the poor law there was no reason for you to sit and beg because you were entitled to have your destitution relieved, whatever it was.'

Opinions vary, and many of the old debates run on. In a future where we hope life will improve for the poorest, perhaps we can still learn from the mistakes and achievements of the past.